FINDING
Grace
AFTER
ABORTION
WORKBOOK

Douglas Weiss, Ph.D.

Contents

Welcome!

Welcome to *Finding Grace After Abortion*. You will discover healing that many others have found before you in these pages. Your journey is unique since you are an amazing woman.

I pray that you will do the work before you and receive the gift this work can give you to walk in your destiny in Christ.

You might have feelings, even strong feelings, so I encourage you to have a friend or a Finding Grace group member to be able to talk and share the work as you go on this courageous journey of healing.

If you don't have a local group in your area, I encourage you to join my Finding Grace After Abortion Facebook Group for women. This is a confidential community where you can connect with other women who have walked this path of healing before you and will walk alongside you as you go through this healing process. You can join this group by visiting *www.facebook.com/groups/abortionhealing*.

You deserve to be known, free, and the powerful woman God has made you.

Dough Weiss Ph.P.

Introduction

Session One
Length: 5 Minutes 32 Seconds

This session started with five clear statements. Write these here:

    1. You are l_____.

    2. You are f_____.

    3. This doesn't d_____ y_____.

    4. You can be f_____ to become the woman you were made to be.

    5. You are not d_____ from having a great life.

In the "Before" space, write out your true thoughts and feelings about each of these statements today. Later when you have completed this workbook, come back and write how you feel about these statements in the "After" space.

You are loved.

Before: _____

_____

_____

_____

_____

After: _____

_____

_____

_____

_____

    Finding Grace After Abortion Workbook

You are forgiven.

Before: _____

_____

_____

_____

After: _____

_____

_____

_____

_____

This doesn't define you.

Before: _____

_____

_____

_____

_____

After: _____

_____

_____

_____

You can be free to become the woman you were made to be.

Before: _____

_____

_____

_____

_____

After: _____

_____

_____

_____

_____

You are not disqualified from having a great life.

Before: _____

_____

_____

_____

_____

After: _____

_____

_____

_____

_____

What are the changes in your behavior you can make or have made after doing this work? Write to yourself about these changes:

_____

_____

_____

_____

_____

_____

_____

_____

_____

_____

_____

_____

In this segment there are two types of miracles discussed: 1) instantaneous healings and 2) process healings. Looking back over your life, how have you experienced process healing in any area of your life or relationships?

_____

_____

_____

_____

_____

_____

_____

_____

_____

_____

_____

Session Two
Length: 11 Minutes 07 Seconds

Who you were at the time this decision was made is an important part to acknowledge as a part of your healing journey. In this session, you will be diving deep into who you were at this time of your life and how this may have impacted what happened.

To say that you were t_____ and o_____ at this time would be an understatement.

You have to be c_____ with your own s_____ at that time.

If you could look at this young woman and she was s_____ o_____ than y_____, you would have compassion on her.

Session Notes:

_____

_____

_____

_____

_____

_____

_____

_____

_____

_____

Healing Exercise: Recognizing Your Circumstances

List your circumstances, who you were, and what you were going through when the abortion happened. Consider the list of environmental factors and relationships that you listed above while also including where you were spiritually, emotionally, and socially at that time.

Environmental factors and physical circumstances:

What I was going through:

- _____
- _____
- _____
- _____
- _____
- _____
- _____
- _____

- _____
- _____
- _____
- _____
- _____
- _____
- _____

My relationships:

_____

_____

_____

_____

_____

_____

_____

External pressures or influences:

_____

_____

_____

_____

_____

_____

Who I was:

_____

_____

_____

_____

_____

Now that you have identified these factors that played a part in what you were going through at that time, write more about these circumstances in detail:

_____

_____

_____

_____

_____

_____

_____

_____

_____

_____

_____

_____

_____

_____

_____

_____

_____

_____

_____

_____

_____

_____

_____

_____

_____

_____

_____

_____

After completing, please read this out loud.

_The day I read this out loud was:_____/_____/_____.

Healing Exercise: Identifying Your Feelings

Make a list of the feelings that you were experiencing in that season or in the moments leading up to the abortion. *You can view a feelings list in the appendix of the workbook.*

_____ _____ _____

_____ _____ _____

_____ _____ _____

_____ _____ _____

_____ _____ _____

After completing, please read these feelings out loud.

The day I read this out loud was:_____/_____/_____.

Healing Exercise: Expressing Your Feelings

For each one of your feelings that you listed above. Write a sentence explaining why you felt that way at that time.

_____: _____

_____

_____: _____

_____

_____: _____

_____

_____: _____

_____

_____: _____

_____

_____: _____

_____

_____: _____

_____

_____: _____

_____

_____: _____

_____

_____: _____

_____

_____: _____

_____

_____: _____

_____

_____: _____

_____

_____: _____

_____

After completing, please read this out loud.

The day I read this out loud was:_____/_____/_____.

Healing Exercise: Speaking to the Younger You

Until now, you may have been suppressing the feelings and circumstances surrounding this time. After processing everything you were going through then, write out what it would sound like if you were having compassion on the younger version of yourself. Include how you feel now about this younger version of yourself.

_____

_____

_____

_____

_____

_____

_____

_____

_____

_____

_____

_____

_____

_____

_____

_____

I shared this work with _____ *on* _____/_____/_____.

Reflection

You have done a lot of work already! However, you must be able to truly process all the exercises you have just completed. Please respond to the following questions.

Which exercise evoked the strongest emotions? Explain below.

_____

_____

_____

_____

_____

_____

What insights or revelations emerged as you worked through the exercises?

_____

_____

_____

_____

_____

Reflect on any shifts in your understanding or perception of that period.

_____

_____

_____

_____

_____

When completing both "Feelings" exercises, were there any feelings you hesitated to be honest about or confront? Explore that hesitation below.

_____

_____

_____

_____

_____

_____

Were there any common themes or sentiments that arose as you explored your feelings or the reasons behind abortion? If so, explain them below.

_____

_____

_____

_____

_____

_____

_____

Reflect on any changes in your feelings towards your younger self after completing the "Speaking to the Younger You" exercise.

_____

_____

_____

_____

_____

_____

"For sin shall no longer be your master, because you are not under the law, but under grace."

Romans 6:14 (NIV)

Complete some research and write a few sentences about what the grace of God is and what giving yourself grace would look like.

_____

_____

_____

_____

_____

If you chose to share your work with another individual or in a group, share how this felt below.

_____

_____

_____

_____

_____

How You Made the Decision

Session Three

Length: 4 Minutes 01 Second

Oftentimes, we are presented with situations where we make choices without the best information possible. In this segment, you will be asked to explore the context and beliefs around the time of the conception. Understanding the context surrounding these circumstances will allow you to start processing, healing, and moving forward.

Life is full of d_____.

Sometimes, we don't have all of the i_____ we need to make a great decision.

You likely had no p_____ to get pregnant.

Session Notes:

_____

_____

_____

_____

_____

_____

_____

_____

_____

_____

Reflection

What was your general belief about sex prior to pregnancy?

_____

_____

_____

_____

What was your belief and behavior about preventing pregnancy?

_____

_____

_____

_____

_____

What were the circumstances prior to being sexual with this person?

_____

_____

_____

_____

_____

What were your circumstances with the person you had sex with? (Just met? Short-term relationship? Long-term relationship?)

_____

_____

_____

What were the belief differences (if any) he had about sex or the relationship?

_____

_____

_____

_____

From your perspective, what emotions led you into this sexual relationship?

_____

_____

_____

_____

What did you learn about yourself and your circumstances from answering these questions?

_____

_____

_____

_____

What lessons have you learned from these past events?

_____

_____

_____

_____

Regarding our discussion on behaviors, how did you shift or change behaviors after these circumstances?

_____

_____

_____

_____

_____

How did societal, familial, religious, or cultural expectations influence your beliefs and decisions regarding sex and relationships?

_____

_____

_____

_____

_____

How has your perspective of these beliefs or circumstances evolved over time?

_____

_____

_____

_____

_____

Think about the voices or influences that were loudest during that time. Share how they were or were not truly representative of your innermost beliefs and desires.

_____

_____

_____

_____

As you evaluate your past choices and beliefs, are there any aspects you haven't given a voice to during this time period? If so, share what those are below.

_____

_____

_____

_____

_____

_____

_____

_____

Conclusion

The goal of this segment is to help you get a full perspective of your situation before the abortion happened. It may be painful to revisit these circumstances, but understanding this context will help you as you move into our next chapter.

I shared this work with _____ *on* _____/_____/_____.

Your Pain

Session Four
Length: 3 Minutes 06 Seconds

If I were to ask you about the emotional pain you've experienced because of post-abortion trauma, it might feel impossible for you to identify. This segment is here to guide you gently through acknowledging these painful areas. By peeling back these layers, you will be able to understand the specific sources of your pain, and move forward on your healing journey.

When you experience the t_____ of an abortion, there is going to be

p_____.

People f_____ pain and r_____ to pain very differently, even if the

c_____ that caused the pain are similar.

You are m_____ and you have m_____

w_____.

Session Notes:

_____

_____

_____

_____

_____

_____

_____

Healing Exercise: Processing Your Pain

This segment dives into multi-dimensional layers of pain that can arise after post-abortion trauma. Below, various dimensions of this experience are outlined. Reflect and share the pain you have experienced in each area in the spaces below.

Reputation

_____

_____

_____

_____

Spirituality (your relationship with God)

_____

_____

_____

_____

Spiritually (your relationship with yourself)

_____

_____

_____

_____

Socially

_____

_____

_____

_____

Financially

_____

_____

_____

_____

Sexually

_____

_____

_____

_____

Emotionally

_____

_____

_____

_____

Self-Esteem

_____

_____

_____

_____

Sexual Esteem

_____

_____

_____

_____

Your Beauty

_____

_____

_____

Your Body

_____

_____

_____

Romantically in Relationships

_____

_____

_____

Your Future

_____

_____

_____

Educationally

_____

_____

_____

Vocationally

_____

_____

_____

_____

Self-Acceptance

_____

_____

_____

_____

Any others you can think of

_____

_____

_____

_____

_____

_____

_____

_____

_____

_____

_____

Read what you wrote above out loud.

Reflection

As you process the different ways pain has impacted your life, share the current state of your heart. Where are you currently at in this healing process?

_____

_____

_____

_____

_____

_____

Which aspects of your pain brought up the strongest feelings, and why do you think that is?

_____

_____

_____

_____

_____

_____

In what ways do societal or cultural beliefs shape the feelings you've noted in areas like reputation or beauty?

_____

_____

_____

_____

_____

_____

When you think about the pain in various areas, what past beliefs or experiences come to mind that might have influenced those emotions?

_____

_____

_____

_____

_____

Trust in Him at all times, you people; pour out your hearts to him, for God is our refuge.

Psalm 62:8 (NIV)

In the space below, take a moment to communicate with God openly. Share your deepest feelings and the pain you've experienced and continue to bear. He is there to listen and be your refuge.

_____

_____

_____

_____

_____

_____

_____

Read your prayer out loud.

The date I read this prayer out loud was: _____/_____/_____.

The Meaning

Session Five

Length: 7 Minutes 20 Seconds

If I were to ask you about the emotional pain you've experienced because of post-abortion trauma, it might feel impossible for you to identify. This segment is here to guide you gently through acknowledging these painful areas. By peeling back these layers, you will be able to understand the specific sources of your pain and move forward on your healing journey.

Both women believed their m_____ with all their heart.

People give m_____ to events.

M_____ can be f_____ or n_____ f_____.

Once a m_____ is created and believed f_____, facts are not

r_____.

When we a_____ this m_____, we can heal.

If we don't c_____ our faults, we can get s_____.

Session Notes:

_____

_____

_____

_____

_____

Healing Exercise: List your Meanings

In this segment, I share a list of meanings that women have shared with me over the years. Some of these meanings may align with how you perceive your experience, while others may not. Please list the relevant meanings below so you can revisit them during the upcoming healing exercise. There are also additional blanks for you to share meanings that haven't been listed in the video.

Meaning #1 _____   Meaning #14 _____

Meaning #2 _____   Meaning #15 _____

Meaning #3 _____   Meaning #16 _____

Meaning #4 _____   Meaning #17 _____

Meaning #5 _____   Meaning #18 _____

Meaning #6 _____   Meaning #19 _____

Meaning #7 _____   Meaning #20 _____

Meaning #8 _____   Meaning #21 _____

Meaning #9 _____   Meaning #22 _____

Meaning #10 _____   Meaning #23 _____

Meaning #11 _____   Meaning #24 _____

Meaning #12 _____   Meaning #25 _____

Meaning #13 _____   Meaning #26 _____

"If we acknowledge this meaning, we can heal."

-Dr. Weiss

Healing Exercise: Processing Your Meanings

On the previous page, you have identified the meanings that you have given yourself. In the below section, reflect on the meanings that you have given to yourself currently or in the past. Remember, meanings are not always factual, but understanding why we believe the way we do can help us achieve breakthrough. For each meaning you listed above, share why you did or currently attribute this meaning to yourself.

Meaning #1: _____

I still believe this meaning: Yes / No

Why? _____

_____

_____

Meaning #2: _____

I still believe this meaning: Yes / No

Why? _____

_____

_____

Meaning #3: _____

I still believe this meaning: Yes / No

Why? _____

_____

_____

Meaning #4: _____

I still believe this meaning: Yes / No

Why? _____

_____

_____

Meaning #5: _____

I still believe this meaning: Yes / No

Why? _____

_____

_____

Meaning #6: _____

I still believe this meaning: Yes / No

Why? _____

_____

_____

Meaning #7: _____

I still believe this meaning: Yes / No

Why? _____

_____

_____

Meaning #8: _____

I still believe this meaning: Yes / No

Why? _____

_____

_____

Meaning #9: _____

I still believe this meaning: Yes / No

Why? _____

_____

_____

Meaning #10: _____

I still believe this meaning: Yes / No

Why? _____

_____

_____

Meaning #11: _____

I still believe this meaning: Yes / No

Why? _____

_____

_____

Meaning #12: _____

I still believe this meaning: Yes / No

Why? _____

_____

_____

Meaning #13: _____

I still believe this meaning: Yes / No

Why? _____

_____

_____

Meaning #14: _____

I still believe this meaning: Yes / No

Why? _____

_____

_____

Meaning #15: _____

I still believe this meaning: Yes / No

Why? _____

_____

_____

Meaning #16: _____

I still believe this meaning: Yes / No

Why? _____

_____

_____

Meaning #17: _____

I still believe this meaning: Yes / No

Why? _____

_____

_____

Meaning #18: _____

I still believe this meaning: Yes / No

Why? _____

_____

_____

Meaning #19: _____

I still believe this meaning: Yes / No

Why? _____

_____

_____

Meaning #20: _____

I still believe this meaning: Yes / No

Why? _____

_____

_____

Meaning #21: _____

I still believe this meaning: Yes / No

Why? _____

_____

_____

Meaning #22: _____

I still believe this meaning: Yes / No

Why? _____

_____

_____

Meaning #23: _____

I still believe this meaning: Yes / No

Why? _____

_____

_____

Meaning #24: _____

I still believe this meaning: Yes / No

Why? _____

_____

_____

Meaning #25: _____

I still believe this meaning: Yes / No

Why? _____

_____

_____

Meaning #26: _____

I still believe this meaning: Yes / No

Why? _____

_____

_____

Reflection

Share the difference between facts and meanings below.

_____

_____

_____

_____

There was an example of women who processed the same event in completely different ways. Explain why recognizing the meanings you are giving your situation is important:

_____

_____

_____

_____

"Therefore confess your sins to each other and pray for each other so that you may be healed."

James 5:16 (NIV)

Share how this verse applies to you below.

_____

_____

_____

_____

_____

_____

Friends

Session Six
Length: 4 Minutes 25 Seconds

In this segment, I will address some of the unhelpful emotions and thoughts that might have become your companions over time. We will explore what these emotions might look like, how they can impact you, and, most importantly, how you can acknowledge them and let them go. The exercises and reflections in this section are designed to help you break ties with these unwelcome "friends" and move forward toward a place of forgiveness and peace.

Friends are usually people that come into your life to s_____ or c_____ you.

Most abortions are done in s_____.

Session Notes:

_____

_____

_____

_____

_____

_____

_____

_____

_____

_____

_____

Healing Exercise: Identifying "Friends"

In this segment, I discussed some of the "friends" that can come into your life after an abortion. In the space below, write out your thoughts and feelings about each "friend" that has accompanied you on this journey.

Shame - *"I am bad."*

_____

_____

_____

_____

_____

Guilt - *"I have done something bad."*

_____

_____

_____

_____

_____

Fears - *"If anyone knew me, they would not love me."*

_____

_____

_____

_____

_____

Worthlessness - *"I am unworthy of..."*

_____

_____

_____

_____

_____

Self-doubt - *"I am undeserving of..."*

_____

_____

_____

Any other "friends" that were not listed.

_____

_____

_____

_____

_____

_____

_____

_____

It's time to dive deep. Share the purpose of each of these "friends" in your life below.

Shame - *"I am bad."*

_____

_____

_____

_____

Guilt - *"I have done something bad."*

_____

_____

_____

_____

Fears - *"If anyone knew me, they would not love me."*

_____

_____

_____

_____

Worthlessness - *"I am unworthy of..."*

_____

_____

_____

_____

Self-doubt - *"I am undeserving of..."*

_____

_____

_____

_____

Any other "friends" that were not listed.

_____

_____

_____

_____

Healing Exercise: The Role "Friends" Play

It's important to recognize the role that these "friends" play in our lives. Maybe they shared an ongoing narrative we were telling ourselves or maybe there's another reason why we have allowed them to be a part of our journey. In the spaces provided on the next pages, write a thank you letter to these "friends".

Shame - *"I am bad."*

_____

_____

_____

_____

_____

_____

_____

_____

_____

_____

_____

_____

_____

_____

_____

_____

_____

_____

_____

_____

Guilt - *"I have done something bad."*

_____

_____

_____

_____

_____

_____

_____

_____

_____

_____

_____

_____

_____

_____

_____

_____

_____

_____

_____

_____

_____

_____

Fears - *"If anyone knew me, they would not love me."*

_____

_____

_____

_____

_____

_____

_____

_____

_____

_____

_____

_____

_____

_____

_____

_____

_____

_____

_____

_____

_____

_____

Worthlessness - *"I am unworthy of..."*

_____

_____

_____

_____

_____

_____

_____

_____

_____

_____

_____

_____

_____

_____

_____

_____

_____

_____

_____

_____

_____

_____

Self-doubt - *"I am undeserving of..."*

_____

_____

_____

_____

_____

_____

_____

_____

_____

_____

_____

_____

_____

_____

_____

_____

_____

_____

_____

_____

_____

Any other "friends" that were not listed.

_____

_____

_____

_____

_____

_____

_____

_____

_____

_____

_____

_____

_____

_____

_____

_____

_____

_____

_____

_____

_____

_____

_____

Healing Exercise: Saying Goodbye

Now that we have processed how these "friends" have been a part of our lives, it is time to say goodbye. Using the following pages, write a goodbye letter to these friends.

Shame - *"I am bad."*

_____

_____

_____

_____

_____

_____

_____

_____

_____

_____

_____

_____

_____

_____

_____

_____

_____

_____

Guilt - *"I have done something bad."*

_____

_____

_____

_____

_____

_____

_____

_____

_____

_____

_____

_____

_____

_____

_____

_____

_____

_____

_____

_____

_____

_____

Fears - *"If anyone knew me, they would not love me."*

_____

_____

_____

_____

_____

_____

_____

_____

_____

_____

_____

_____

_____

_____

_____

_____

_____

_____

_____

_____

_____

_____

Worthlessness - *"I am unworthy of..."*

_____

_____

_____

_____

_____

_____

_____

_____

_____

_____

_____

_____

_____

_____

_____

_____

_____

_____

_____

_____

_____

_____

Self-doubt - *"I am undeserving of..."*

_____

_____

_____

_____

_____

_____

_____

_____

_____

_____

_____

_____

_____

_____

_____

_____

_____

_____

_____

_____

Any other "friends" that were not listed.

_____

_____

_____

_____

_____

_____

_____

_____

_____

_____

_____

_____

_____

_____

_____

_____

_____

_____

_____

_____

Now I want you to read each thank you and corresponding goodbye letter out loud. For example, read the Shame "thank you" letter first then read the Shame "goodbye" letter after. This may take some time, but it is a worthwhile step in your healing journey.

The day I read these letter out loud was:_____/_____/_____.

Reflection

It's time to process this exercise. What were you feeling before, during, and after this exercise? Write down what you experienced after writing and reading out loud the thank you and goodbye letters.

Before: _____

_____

_____

_____

_____

_____

During: _____

_____

_____

_____

_____

_____

After: _____

_____

_____

_____

_____

Over the next month, keep track of any "friends" that have tried to revisit and who you called when they do.

Week 1: "Friends" that have visited

Shame - *"I am bad."*

_____

_____

_____

_____

_____

Guilt - *"I have done something bad."*

_____

_____

_____

_____

_____

Fears - *"If anyone knew me, they would not love me."*

_____

_____

_____

_____

_____

Worthlessness - *"I am unworthy of..."*

_____

_____

_____

_____

_____

Self-doubt - *"I am undeserving of..."*

_____

_____

_____

_____

Any other "friends" that were not listed.

_____

_____

_____

_____

_____

Week 2: "Friends" that have visited

Shame - *"I am bad."*

_____

_____

_____

_____

_____

Guilt - *"I have done something bad."*

_____

_____

_____

_____

_____

Fears - _"If anyone knew me, they would not love me."_

_____

_____

_____

_____

Worthlessness - _"I am unworthy of..."_

_____

_____

_____

_____

Self-doubt - _"I am undeserving of..."_

_____

_____

_____

_____

Any other "friends" that were not listed.

_____

_____

_____

_____

_____

Week 3: "Friends" that have visited

Shame - *"I am bad."*

_____

_____

_____

_____

_____

Guilt - *"I have done something bad."*

_____

_____

_____

_____

_____

Fears - *"If anyone knew me, they would not love me."*

_____

_____

_____

_____

_____

Worthlessness - *"I am unworthy of..."*

_____

_____

_____

_____

_____

_____

Self-doubt - _"I am undeserving of..."_

_____

_____

_____

_____

Any other "friends" that were not listed.

_____

_____

_____

_____

Week 4: "Friends" that have visited

Shame - _"I am bad."_

_____

_____

_____

_____

Guilt - _"I have done something bad."_

_____

_____

_____

_____

_____

Fears - *"If anyone knew me, they would not love me."*

_____

_____

_____

_____

Worthlessness - *"I am unworthy of..."*

_____

_____

_____

_____

_____

Self-doubt - *"I am undeserving of..."*

_____

_____

_____

_____

_____

Any other "friends" that were not listed.

_____

_____

_____

_____

Week 5: "Friends" that have visited

Shame - *"I am bad."*

_____

_____

_____

_____

_____

Guilt - *"I have done something bad."*

_____

_____

_____

_____

_____

Fears - *"If anyone knew me, they would not love me."*

_____

_____

_____

_____

Worthlessness - *"I am unworthy of..."*

_____

_____

_____

_____

_____

Self-doubt - *"I am undeserving of..."*

_____

_____

_____

_____

_____

Any other "friends" that were not listed.

_____

_____

_____

_____

_____

Now that you have tracked the "friends" that have visited you over the last four weeks, it's time for some evaluation.

Were you surprised by the frequency of your "friends" visiting? Why or why not?

_____

_____

_____

_____

_____

Document any shifts in frequency of "friend" visits over the last four weeks.

_____

_____

_____

_____

Write three statements or Bible verses that you can use against these "friends" when they visit:

1. _____

_____

2. _____

_____

3. _____

_____

Forgiving Yourself

Session Seven
Length: 5 Minutes 22 Seconds

Forgiveness is a key idea of our faith - This includes forgiving ourselves. In this session, I want to walk you through a powerful exercise that can help you navigate forgiving yourself.

Session Notes:

_____

_____

_____

_____

_____

_____

Healing Exercise: Chairs

After you have followed the instructions of this exercise in the video, record what you said in each chair.

Chair 1: *As myself*

_____

_____

_____

_____

_____

_____

_____

_____

_____

Chair 2: *As myself responding*

_____

_____

_____

_____

_____

_____

_____

_____

Chair 3: *As myself saying "thank you"* **if** *I forgave*

_____

_____

_____

_____

_____

_____

_____

_____

_____

_____

Reflection

If you were able to forgive yourself, write down what you felt and experienced in this exercise.

_____

_____

_____

_____

_____

_____

_____

It is possible you were not able to forgive yourself yet. Write down what you experienced in this exercise.

_____

_____

_____

_____

_____

If you weren't ready to forgive yourself, that's okay. It may take some time, but I encourage you to process why you might not be ready to forgive yourself yet. Please write your thoughts and feelings about this below.

_____

_____

_____

_____

Asking Forgiveness from God

Session Eight

Length: 3 Minutes 03 Seconds

In this important segment, you will explore the significance of seeking God's forgiveness. This is a pivotal step in your healing journey. The exercise in this segment allows you to release the burden of guilt and shame so you can freely continue to walk in your relationship with God.

Session Notes:

_____

_____

_____

_____

_____

_____

_____

Healing Exercise: Chairs

After you have followed the instructions of this exercise in the video, record what you said in each chair.

Chair One: *Being myself*

_____

_____

_____

_____

_____

_____

_____

_____

_____

Chair Two: *Being God/Jesus*

_____

_____

_____

_____

_____

_____

_____

_____

Chair Three: *Me responding to God/Jesus*

_____

_____

_____

_____

_____

_____

_____

_____

_____

Reflection

What did you feel or experience doing this exercise?

_____

_____

_____

_____

_____

_____

_____

_____

_____

Reflect on any moments of difficulty you encountered while asking for forgiveness. What do you think was at the root of those feelings?

_____

_____

_____

_____

_____

_____

_____

_____

_____

_____

_____

In what ways has asking for God's forgiveness impacted your view of yourself?

_____

_____

_____

_____

_____

_____

_____

_____

_____

Reflect on any moments of grace or relief you experienced during this exercise. How can you carry these moments with you as you continue your healing journey?

_____

_____

_____

_____

_____

_____

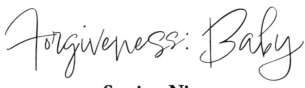

Forgiveness: Baby

Session Nine
Length: 4 Minutes 15 Seconds

In this healing exercise, you will be creating a space to reflect and connect with your deepest feelings regarding the abortion. It might be challenging, but it's a critical part of your journey towards healing. I encourage you to take this exercise at your own pace and remember that feeling a wide range of emotions is okay.

Session Notes:

_____

_____

_____

_____

_____

_____

_____

Healing Exercise: Chairs

After you have followed the instructions of this exercise in the video, record what you said in each chair. If there is more than one baby, do the exercise with each.

Chair One: *Being myself and asking baby for forgiveness*

_____

_____

_____

_____

_____

_____

_____

Chair Two: *Being the baby*

_____

_____

_____

_____

_____

_____

Chair Three: *As me responding to baby*

_____

_____

_____

_____

_____

_____

_____

Baby 1

_____

_____

_____

_____

_____

_____

_____

_____

Baby 2

_____

_____

_____

_____

_____

_____

_____

Baby 3

_____

_____

_____

_____

_____

_____

_____

_____

_____

Reflection

What did you feel or experience overall after doing this exercise?

_____

_____

_____

_____

_____

_____

_____

_____

_____

Were there any unexpected emotions that you experienced during the exercise? If so, write them below.

_____

_____

_____

_____

_____

_____

_____

_____

_____

_____

What part of this exercise felt most significant or meaningful to you?

_____

_____

_____

_____

_____

_____

_____

_____

Is there anything you learned from this exercise that you would like to carry forward in your healing journey? If so, share below.

_____

_____

_____

_____

_____

_____

_____

_____

_____

Tell Someone

Session Ten

Length: 3 Minutes 52 Seconds

Telling someone about your abortion might feel scary, but it can be a very powerful step toward healing. When we share our stories, we break the chains of guilt and shame that often keep us isolated. By confiding in a trustworthy friend or family member, you not only release the burden you've been carrying but also open the door to receive compassion and support.

You can be l_____ even though you're k_____.

If you keep your secrets to yourself, you can stay s_____.

Abortion is one of the deepest s_____ the soul can have.

You can start freeing yourself by telling s_____.

When we let the secret out, we allow healing in our h_____.

Session Notes:

_____

_____

_____

_____

_____

_____

_____

_____

Healing Exercises

What is/are the reason(s) you haven't told anyone?

_____

_____

_____

_____

_____

If you have yet to tell someone, who would be the top three people you would choose?

1. _____

2. _____

3. _____

When will you contact one of these people to tell them your story? _____

When did you tell someone?_____/_____/_____.

Reflection

What did you feel before, during, and after sharing with this person?

Before:

_____

_____

_____

_____

_____

_____

_____

_____

_____

_____

During:

_____

_____

_____

_____

_____

_____

_____

_____

_____

After:

_____

_____

_____

_____

_____

_____

_____

_____

_____

What were your initial feelings or hesitations that you had when you were asked to share your story?

_____

_____

_____

_____

_____

_____

In what ways did holding on to this secret affect you in the past?

_____

_____

_____

_____

_____

_____

Share any moments that stood out to you or felt particularly impactful throughout the exercise.

_____

_____

_____

_____

_____

_____

When I See You

Session Eleven

Length: 4 Minutes 06 Seconds

As Christians, we hold onto the promise of seeing our loved ones again in heaven. This includes the children we never knew here on Earth. In this session, we will explore the understanding that, as a Christian, you will one day reunite with your child in heaven. Here, we'll reflect on this hope and its implications for your healing journey.

Your baby has been living in h_____.

If you go to h_____ you are g_____ to see your child again.

P_____ yourself for this moment.

You will see your child again – and when you do, you will have so much j_____.

Session Notes:

_____

_____

_____

_____

_____

_____

_____

_____

_____

_____

Healing Exercises

Write a letter you would like to say to your child when you meet him or her in heaven:

_____

_____

_____

_____

_____

_____

_____

_____

_____

_____

_____

_____

_____

_____

_____

_____

_____

_____

_____

_____

_____

_____

_____

_____

_____

_____

_____

_____

_____

_____

_____

_____

_____

_____

_____

_____

_____

_____

_____

_____

_____

_____

_____

_____

_____

_____

_____

Now, read your letter aloud to a trusted friend or your group.

I shared my letter with _____ on _____ / _____ / _____.

Reflection

What did you feel when you were writing the letter to your child?

_____

_____

_____

_____

_____

_____

_____

_____

_____

_____

Reflecting on your letter, what key messages or feelings did you want to convey?

_____

_____

_____

_____

_____

_____

_____

_____

_____

_____

In what ways has envisioning a reunion with your baby in heaven influenced your perspective on forgiveness and grace?

_____

_____

_____

_____

_____

_____

_____

_____

_____

What did you experience or feel when you shared your letter?

_____

_____

_____

_____

_____

_____

_____

_____

_____

What did you experience or feel when reading the letter to another person or your group?

_____

_____

_____

_____

_____

_____

_____

_____

_____

Did this exercise change your relationship with the concept of heaven or your spiritual beliefs in any way?

_____

_____

_____

_____

_____

_____

_____

_____

_____

_____

Your Salvation

Throughout this journey, you may have wondered about your eternal destiny and whether you will meet your baby in heaven. I want to share with you a simple yet life-changing truth. Jesus Christ came into this world for each one of us. He died on the cross to pay the price for all our sins, including the choices and actions we deeply regret. His love and forgiveness are available to everyone, regardless of your past.

If you haven't yet made a decision to follow Jesus and are uncertain about your relationship with Him, know that it's never too late. Asking Jesus for forgiveness, turning away from past mistakes, and deciding to live for Him is the pathway to experiencing His grace and assurance of eternal life. This decision means that you can have confidence in your salvation and hope to be reunited with your child in heaven. If you're ready to make this decision, you can start by praying, asking Jesus to forgive your sins, and inviting Him to be the Lord of your life.

To keep growing in your faith, connecting with others who share your beliefs is helpful. Consider joining a local church where you can learn more and find support. They can guide you on what to do next as a new believer.

For further resources and information on your journey towards being saved by Jesus Christ, visit **www.healingtimeministries.com/next-steps.**

Remember, your walk with God is an ongoing process, and there are many who are ready to support you along the way.

Dear Jesus

Session Twelve
Length: 1 Minute 57 Seconds

You can feel comfort in believing your child is in the care of a loving God. In this segment, we'll reflect on the concept that your child has been in the tender care of Jesus. While we cannot comprehend all the mysteries of heaven, you can hold the faith that there is a special place in heaven where your child is cherished and loved.

God is a F_____ to the f_____.

God is not only a good G_____, He is a good f_____.

When your child entered eternity, J_____ met your child and has been a great f_____ to your child.

Session Notes:

_____

_____

_____

_____

_____

_____

_____

_____

_____

Healing Exercise: Thanking Jesus

Use the space below to write a letter to Jesus thanking Him for all He has done for your child all these years.

_____

_____

_____

_____

_____

_____

_____

_____

_____

_____

_____

_____

_____

_____

_____

_____

_____

_____

_____

_____

_____

_____

_____

_____

_____

_____

_____

_____

_____

_____

Reflection

How did the process of writing a letter of thanks to Jesus for taking care of your child make you feel, and what emotions arose during the exercise?

_____

_____

_____

_____

_____

_____

_____

_____

_____

_____

_____

Can't Be Done

Session Thirteen
Length: 4 Minutes 08 Seconds

As believers, understanding the eternal nature of our souls is critical. As we explore this truth, we recognize that although our loved ones may no longer be with us physically, their spirits endure beyond this life. In this session, I will discuss the eternal existence of the human soul and offer a unique perspective that can help bridge the gap between our earthly experiences and the everlasting life that awaits us.

God has never made m_____ to d_____.

We are all e_____ beings made in t_____.

H_____ itself can't destroy a human s_____.

Humans cannot be k_____.

Your child was eternal the moment God gave him or her l_____.

Your child is i_____.

Session Notes:

_____

_____

_____

_____

_____

_____

_____

_____

Reflection

In this session, you heard the teaching on Indestructible. What are some of the key points you learned from this teaching?

1. _____

_____

2. _____

_____

3. _____

_____

4. _____

_____

5. _____

_____

What are your thoughts about all of us being made indestructible?

_____

_____

_____

_____

How has this idea impacted you as it regards to your child never being destroyed?

_____

_____

_____

_____

_____

Gifts

Session 14

Length: 3 Minutes 06 Seconds

Shame tries to anchor us down, making us feel unworthy of pursuing our God-given callings and gifts. Yet, it's crucial to understand that our past does not disqualify us from the future God has planned for our lives. This segment focuses on embracing the gifts you've been given and stepping into your calling, despite your past, knowing that you are still equipped and called to make a meaningful impact.

When things happen in our life, how we t_____ about them is very important.

The scripture is very powerful when you b_____ it and e_____ it.

Your abortion did not in any way d_____ you from your calling.

You are more e_____ to help women in this unique way than you ever have been before.

Never believe your abortion sidelines you from your d_____.

You will always be y_____.

Take your c_____ and your g_____ very seriously.

Session Notes:

_____

_____

_____

_____

_____

Reflection

Utilizing the gifts that God has given you is important. What do you see as your g
from God?

1. _____

_____

2. _____

_____

3. _____

_____

4. _____

_____

5. _____

_____

6. _____

_____

7. _____

_____

8. _____

_____

As you look at your life, have you in any way allowed your history to slow you down or make you feel not good enough to develop or express your gifts? If so, explain.

_____

_____

_____

_____

What do you think or feel about the statement "to fulfill your destiny is the greatest gift you can give this child"?

_____

_____

_____

_____

_____

_____

_____

_____

What would your life look like if you were developing or utilizing your gifts?

_____

_____

_____

_____

_____

_____

_____

_____

_____

Who can hold you accountable to start developing or utilizing your gifts if you have not been? _____

The day I talked to this person and came up with a plan was_____/_____/_____.

Talk to the Devil

Session Fifteen
Length: 1 Minute 55 Seconds

The healing journey often includes recognizing the spiritual battles we face as believers. Knowing that the enemy seeks opportunities to disrupt our progress with lies and shame is essential. In this segment, you will learn the importance of having a strategic plan to defend against these attacks, ensuring you can remain steadfast in the truth.

We all have an e_____ as followers of Christ.

The devil likes to give us:

F_____ C_____,

S_____, and

G_____.

The devil likes to mess with our e_____ and m_____ to sidetrack us.

You need to be prepared with s_____ and t_____ to combat attacks that occur.

Session Notes:

_____

_____

_____

_____

_____

Healing Exercise: Preparing Yourself

What are the scriptures you can use when the devil attacks you?

1. _____

_____

2. _____

_____

3. _____

_____

4. _____

_____

5. _____

_____

Reflection

What are some attacks that the devil seems to use on you?

1. _____

_____

2. _____

_____

3. _____

_____

4. _____

_____

5. _____

_____

What are things you can say back to the devil when these attacks happen?

1. _____

_____

2. _____

_____

3. _____

_____

4. _____

_____

5. _____

_____

Who can you talk to when you're struggling with the devil's attacks?

_____.

Not Alone

Session Sixteen

Length: 2 Minutes 06 Seconds

As you walked through this process of finding grace, who are some of the people you shared your journey with?

1. _____

2. _____

3. _____

4. _____

5. _____

I want you to go back to the very first page (5) of this workbook and write out your responses to the statements of beliefs where it says after completing the workbook.

I finished on this date:_____ /_____ /_____.

As we close the pages of this workbook, I want to take a moment to express my gratitude that you allowed me to walk alongside you on this remarkable journey. I would love to hear more about your journey as you have walked through this series. You can send me an email at *heart2heart@xc.org* to share your testimony about how your heart shifted during this time. I would love to connect with you and your group members in my Finding Grace After Abortion Facebook Group. This is a private space for you to connect with other women while offering and receiving support. To join the group, visit: *www.facebook.com/groups/abortionhealing.*

I am incredibly proud of the steps you've taken and excited to see the impact you'll make. Thank you for embracing this journey with an open heart.

Where the Spirit of the Lord is there is freedom!
YOU ARE FREE!

Appendix

Feelings List

Abandoned	Badgered	Competent	Destroyed	Friendly
Abused	Baited	Competitive	Different	Frightened
Aching	Bashful	Complacent	Dirty	Frustrated
Accepted	Battered	Complete	Disenchanted	Full
Accused	Beaten	Confident	Disgusted	Funny
Accepting	Beautiful	Confused	Disinterested	Furious
Admired	Belligerent	Considerate	Dispirited	Gabby
Adored	Belittled	Consumed	Distressed	Generous
Adventurous	Bereaved	Content	Distrustful	Gentle
Affectionate	Betrayed	Cool	Distrusted	Genuine
Afraid	Bewildered	Courageous	Disturbed	Giddy
Agony	Blamed	Courteous	Dominated	Giving
Alienated	Blaming	Coy	Domineering	Goofy
Aloof	Bonded	Crabby	Doomed	Grateful
Aggravated	Bored	Cranky	Doubtful	Greedy
Agreeable	Bothered	Crazy	Dreadful	Grief
Aggressive	Brave	Creative	Eager	Grim
Alive	Breathless	Critical	Ecstatic	Grimy
Alone	Bristling	Criticized	Edgy	Grouchy
Amazed	Broken-up	Cross	Edified	Grumpy
Amused	Bruised	Crushed	Elated	Hard
Angry	Bubbly	Cuddly	Embarrassed	Harried
Anguished	Burdened	Curious	Empowered	Hassled
Annoyed	Burned	Cut	Empty	Healthy
Anxious	Callous	Damned	Enraged	Helpful
Apart	Calm	Dangerous	Enraptured	Helpless
Apathetic	Capable	Daring	Enthusiastic	Hesitant
Apologetic	Captivated	Dead	Enticed	High
Appreciated	Carefree	Deceived	Esteemed	Hollow
Appreciative	Careful	Deceptive	Exasperated	Honest
Apprehensive	Careless	Defensive	Excited	Hopeful
Appropriate	Caring	Delicate	Exhilarated	Hopeless
Approved	Cautious	Delighted	Exposed	Horrified
Argumentative	Certain	Demeaned	Fake	Hostile
Aroused	Chased	Demoralized	Fascinated	Humiliated
Astonished	Cheated	Dependent	Feisty	Hurried
Assertive	Cheerful	Depressed	Ferocious	Hurt
Attached	Childlike	Deprived	Foolish	Hyper
Attacked	Choked-up	Deserted	Forced	Ignorant
Attentive	Close	Desirable	Forceful	Ignored
Attractive	Cold	Desired	Forgiven	Immature
Aware	Comfortable	Despair	Forgotten	Impatient
Awestruck	Comforted	Despondent	Free	Important

Feelings List

Impotent	Nurtured	Remember	Sorry	Unapproachable
Impressed	Nuts	Removed	Spacey	Unaware
Incompetent	Obsessed	Repulsed	Special	Uncertain
Incomplete	Offended	Repulsive	Spiteful	Uncomfortable
Independent	Open	Resentful	Spontaneous	Under control
Insecure	Ornery	Resistant	Squelched	Understanding
Innocent	Out of control	Responsible	Starved	Understood
Insignificant	Overcome	Responsive	Stiff	Undesirable
Insincere	Overjoyed	Repressed	Stifled	Unfriendly
Isolated	Overpowered	Respected	Stimulated	Ungrateful
Inspired	Overwhelmed	Restless	Strangled	Unified
Insulted	Pampered	Revolved	Strong	Unhappy
Interested	Panicked	Riled	Stubborn	Unimpressed
Intimate	Paralyzed	Rotten	Stuck	Unsafe
Intolerant	Paranoid	Ruined	Stunned	Unstable
Involved	Patient	Sad	Stupid	Upset
Irate	Peaceful	Safe	Subdued	Uptight
Irrational	Pensive	Satiated	Submissive	Used
Irked	Perceptive	Satisfied	Successful	Useful
Irresponsible	Perturbed	Scared	Suffocated	Useless
Irritable	Phony	Scolded	Sure	Unworthy
Irritated	Pleasant	Scorned	Sweet	Validated
Isolated	Pleased	Scrutinized	Sympathy	Valuable
Jealous	Positive	Secure	Tainted	Valued
Jittery	Powerless	Sedentary	Tearful	Victorious
Joyous	Present	Seduced	Tender	Violated
Lively	Precious	Self-centered	Tense	Violent
Lonely	Pressured	Self-conscious	Terrific	Voluptuous
Loose	Pretty	Selfish	Terrified	Vulnerable
Lost	Proud	Separated	Thrilled	Warm
Loving	Pulled apart	Sensitive	Ticked	Wary
Low	Put down	Sexy	Tickled	Weak
Lucky	Puzzled	Shattered	Tight	Whipped
Lustful	Quarrelsome	Shocked	Timid	Whole
Mad	Queary	Shot down	Tired	Wicked
Maudlin	Quiet	Shy	Tolerant	Wild
Malicious	Raped	Sickened	Tormented	Willing
Mean	Ravished	Silly	Torn	Wiped out
Miserable	Raw	Sincere	Tortured	Wishful
Misunderstood	Real	Sinking	Touched	Withdrawn
Moody	Refreshed	Smart	Trapped	Wonderful
Morose	Regretful	Smothered	Tremendous	Worried
Mournful	Rejected	Smug	Tricked	Worthy
Mystified	Rejuvenated	Sneaky	Trusted	Wounded
Nasty	Rejecting	Snowed	Trustful	Young
Nervous	Relaxed	Soft	Trusting	Zapped
Nice	Relieved	Solid	Ugly	
Numb	Remarkable	Solitary	Unacceptable	

DOWNLOAD

DVD COPY

The Indestructible series gives you a foundational understanding about your innate design as God's child. Addiction, betrayal, abuse, or neglect can all cause trials in our lives that can trigger feelings of worthlessness and defeat. God's Word reveals that your soul is not capable of being destroyed. Once you recognize and embrace your indestructible nature, you can change how you think, feel, and believe about your past, present, and future!

In this teaching you will learn that:

- God created you to be indestructible
- Your eternal nature started at birth
- Your trials, struggles, and tribulations are not capable of destroying you
- Every human being is indestructible and faces an eternal choice

To order this resource, visit www.drdougweiss.com/store or call 719.278.3708

CHRISTIAN RESOURCES

Indestructible

$29.00

The *Indestructible* series gives you a foundational understanding of your innate design as God's child. Addiction, betrayal, trauma, and abuse or neglect can all cause trials in our lives that can trigger feelings of worthlessness and defeat. God's Word reveals that your soul is not capable of being destroyed. Once you recognize and embrace your indestructible nature, you can change how you think, feel, and believe about your past, present, and future!

Emotional Fitness

$16.95

Everyone has an unlimited number of emotions, but few have been trained to identify, choose, communicate, and master them. More than a guide for gaining emotional fitness and mastery, in these pages you will find a pathway to a much more fulfilling life.

Worthy

WORKBOOK: $29.95/DVD: $29.95

The Worthy Exercises & Stepbook and DVD are designed for a 12-week study. Here is a path that anyone can take to process their self-worth and feel worthy again! Follow this path, and you, too, will make the journey from worthless to worthy, just as others have.

Lover Spouse

$13.95

This book provides guidelines to lead a prosperous married life and is helpful for anyone wanting to know more about what the Lord Almighty desires for your love and marriage. Featured with practical tips and foundational relationship skills, the information offered in this book will guide couples through the process of creating an intimate Christian marriage based on a solid biblical worldview.

For more information, visit www.drdougweiss.com/store or call 719.278.3708

Recovery for Everyone

BOOK :$22.95/DVD: $99.00/WORKBOOK: $39.95/STEPBOOK: $14.95

Recovery for Everyone helps addicts fight and recover from any addiction they are facing. Learn truths and gain a biblical understanding to break the strongholds in your life.

You will also find an explanation as to how an addiction may have become a part of your life and details as to how you can walk the path to recovery. You will find a roadmap to help you begin and navigate an incredible journey toward freedom. Then you can become part of the solution and even help others get free as well.

Born for War

$29.95

Born for War teaches practical tools to defeat these sexual landmines and offers scriptural truths that empower young men to desire success in the war thrust upon them. In this DVD, he equips this generation to win the war for their destiny. It also includes one session for parents to support their son through this battle.

Letters to My Daughter

$14.95

A gift for your daughter as she enters college. *Letters to My Daughter* includes Dr. Doug Weiss' daily letters to his daughter during her first year of college. The letters are about life, God, boys, relationships, and being successful in college and life in general.

Get A Grip

BOOK: $19.99

The *Get a Grip* book gives you the power to take control of things that are controlling you. It helps readers discover the source of their behaviors, learn how to let go of secrets and become an accountable and responsible adult who is finally empowered to live a life of freedom.

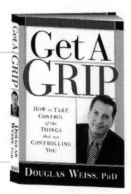

PRODUCTS FOR INTIMACY ANOREXIA

Helping My Spouse Heal from My Intimacy Anorexia Video Course

$99.00

Are you struggling to validate your spouse's pain from Intimacy Anorexia and help them begin to heal? For the spouse of an intimacy anorexic, the pain is excruciating and sometimes even debilitating. This course is for the intimacy anorexic who is aware of their behaviors and wants to transition into a connected, intimate relationship with their spouse.

Intimacy Anorexia

BOOK: $22.95/DVD: $69.95

This hidden addiction is destroying so many marriages today. In your hands is the first antidote for someone with intimacy anorexia to turn the pages on this addiction process. Excerpts from intimacy anorexics and their spouses help this book become clinically helpful and personal in its impact to communicate hope and healing for the intimacy anorexic and the marriage.

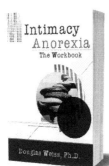

Intimacy Anorexia: The Workbook

$39.95

Intimacy Anorexia is a hidden addiction that is destroying many marriages today. Within the pages of this workbook, you will find more than 100 practical and empowering exercises to guide you through your personal recovery towards intimacy. Dr. Douglas Weiss has been successfully counseling intimacy anorexics for many years in his practice.

Intimacy Anorexia: The Steps

$14.95

This workbook follows in the tradition of the Twelve-Steps breaking down the various principles for readers so that they can experience freedom from intimacy anorexia. It is our hope that you will join the millions who have received help in their personal recovery using these Twelve-Steps.

Pain for Love

$29.95

Pain For Love describes in detail one of the most insidious strategies of an intimacy anorexic with their spouse. This dynamic is experienced by many who are married to an intimacy anorexic. This paradigm can empower the spouse and help them stop participating in a pain for love dynamic in their marriage.

For more information, visit www.drdougweiss.com/store or call 719.278.3708

Sin of Withholding

$49.95

This video is the first to address the Biblical foundation of the sin of withholding in believers' hearts. The practical application in marriage addressing Intimacy Anorexia is also interwoven in this revelational teaching on the Sin of Withholding. Once a believer is free of this sin, their walk with the Lord and their fruit towards others can increase expediently.

Narcissism Sex Addiction & Intimacy Anorexia

$29.95

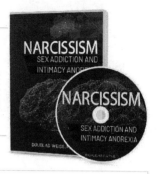

The profound information that you will learn in this video will help you fairly evaluate your specific situation for narcissism, which will help you develop a treatment plan to address the issue you are dealing with at its core. Having this clarity can help expedite the healing process for the sex addict, intimacy anorexic, and the spouse, as they are able to tackle the real issue at hand.

Married & Alone

BOOK: $14.95/DVD: $49.95

The impact of being married and alone is very real. Dr. Weiss explains why and will help you to start a journey of recovery from living with a spouse with intimacy anorexia. My hope is that whatever reason you are watching this DVD you realize that you are worthy of being loved, whether your spouse has decided to pursue recovery or has chosen his or her intimacy anorexia over you.

Married and Alone: Healing Exercises for Spouses

$39.95

This workbook is designed to help the spouse heal from the impact of their relationship with an intimacy anorexic, which may have been experienced over years or decades. The addiction patterns of an alcoholic, gambler, overeater, sex addict, or intimacy anorexic have a direct impact on their spouse's life in so many ways.

Married and Alone: The Twelve Step Guide

$14.95

This book follows in the tradition of the Twelve-Steps by breaking down the various principles for each reader so that they can experience the discovery of the Twelve-Step promises. It is our hope that you will join the millions who have received help in their recovery by using these Twelve-Steps. These Steps can further your healing and recovery from your spouse's Intimacy Anorexia.

For more information, visit www.drdougweiss.com/store or call 719.278.3708

PRODUCTS FOR PARTNER RECOVERY

Partners: Healing From His Addiction

$22.95

Partners: Healing from His Addiction offers real hope that you can heal from his sexual addiction. After presenting statistics and personal stories, it will walk you down the path to reclaim your life, your voice, and your power to be who you are without the impact of his addiction.

Partner's Recovery Guide: 100 Empowering Exercises

$39.95

The *Partners Recovery Guide: 100 Empowering Exercises* guide was borne out of the latest in research on the effects on a woman who has lived with a sexual addict. This workbook will take you down the clear path of healing from the devastating impact of his sex addiction and accompany you along your entire journey.

Beyond Love: A 12 Step Guide for Partners

$14.95

Beyond Love is an interactive workbook that allows partners of sex addicts to gain insight and strength through working the Twelve Steps. This book can be used for individual purposes or as a group study workbook.

Partner Betrayal Trauma

BOOK: $22.95/DVD: $65.95

Partner Betrayal Trauma is an outstanding guide about becoming stronger every day and getting past the trauma of betrayal. The pain and experience of betrayal impacts all of your being and relationships. Fix your broken heart, help your relationships, and reclaim your marriage with the necessary strategies for your recovery.

Partner Betrayal Trauma: The Workbook

$39.95

In this workbook by Dr. Weiss, you will process and work through your partner betrayal trauma so you can overcome it and be the strongest version of yourself. This is an excellent guide for those struggling to overcome the past trauma of a betrayal in their relationship.

For more information, visit www.drdougweiss.com/store or call 719.278.3708

Partner Betrayal Trauma: Step Guide

$14.95

This is an excellent step-by-step guide for those struggling to overcome the past trauma of a betrayal in their relationship. You will gain insight from a psychologist who has worked with countless betrayed women for over 30 years to provide them with the support they need to come out the other side healed, whole and ready to move forward.

He Needs To Change, Dr. Weiss

$29.95

The *He Needs To Change, Dr. Weiss* video addresses the pain, trauma, and betrayal women experience because of their partner's sex addiction, betrayal, and/or intimacy anorexia. In this DVD, Dr. Weiss addresses the issue of change that he has explained to thousands of women in his office.

Unstuck for Partners

$29.00

The *Unstuck* video is for every woman who has experienced the pain of their partner's sex addiction or intimacy anorexia and feels stuck, confused, frustrated and unable to move on. You didn't sign up for this and honestly, you don't get it! This DVD helps you "get it" so you can process the painful reality you are in and start to live again.

Why Do I Stay, When it Doesn't make Sense

$39.95

In this video, Dr. Doug Weiss utilizes his several decades of experience to give you information and tools that can help you make your decision with mental clarity and confidence. Whether you decide to stay, separate, or divorce, your future can be filled with new opportunities and a life that you genuinely enjoy.

Triggered

$49.00

In the *Triggered* video, Dr. Weiss gives women a repertoire of tools to be successful when a trigger occurs. Triggers are normal for partners of sex addicts, but each woman's triggers are unique and must be navigated in different ways. This video can be a life-changing message which will validate your struggles to heal and help you face the challenges of being triggered after partner betrayal trauma.

PRODUCTS FOR MEN'S RECOVERY

The Final Freedom

BOOK: $22.95

The Final Freedom gives more current information than many professional counselors have today. In addition to informing sex addicts and their partners about sex addiction, it gives hope for recovery. The information provided in this book would cost hundreds of dollars in counseling hours to receive. Many have attested to successful recovery from this information alone.

101 Freedom Exercises

$39.95

This workbook provides tips, principles, survival techniques, and therapeutic homework that have been tested and proven on many recovering sex addicts from all walks of life who have practiced these principles and have maintained their sobriety for many years. Jesus promised us a life of freedom; this book makes this promise a practical journey.

Steps to Freedom

$14.95

The Twelve Steps of Recovery have become a major influence in the restoration of this country from the age-old problem of alcohol and substance abuse. This book follows the tradition of the Twelve Steps from a Christian perspective, breaking down the various principles for each reader so that they can experience freedom from sexual addiction.

Helping Her Heal

DVD: $69.95/COMPANION GUIDE: $11.95

The *Helping Her Heal* DVD paired with this companion guide are both vital tools for the man who has struggled with sexual addiction, exposed his marriage to the fallout of betrayal by acting on his urges, and is now seeking how to help his wife heal from the trauma of this devastating discovery.

Disclosure: Preparing and Completing

$39.95

This information about disclosure can help the addict and the spouse navigate these often uncharted and misguided waters, saving the addict and the spouse from unnecessary pain or trauma. This DVD can expedite the understanding of each of the significant processes of disclosure for the addict, the spouse, and the marriage.

Healing Her Heart After Relapse

$29.95

This video is way more than, "He relapses, he does a consequence and moves on." The addict is given real tools to address the emotional damage and repair of her heart as a result of a relapse. Every couple in recovery would do well to have these tools before a potential relapse.

Boundaries: His. Hers. Ours.

$49.95

Boundaries are a healthy, normal, and necessary part of the recovery process for sex addicts, intimacy anorexics, and their spouses. Implementing boundaries in a relationship may seem complicated, but with the proper tools and guidance, you can successfully introduce and implement boundaries in your relationship. In this DVD set, Dr. Doug Weiss answers the clarion call on boundaries by educating and guiding you through this process.

Marriage After Addiction

$29.00

Addiction can have devastating effects on even good marriages. In this DVD you are intelligently guided through the journey you will experience if addiction is part of your marriage story. You will learn important information about the early and later stages of recovery for your marriage.

Shattering Sexualization

$29.95

Dr. Doug Weiss, a Licensed Psychologist who has worked with thousands of men and women struggling with sexualization, will walk you step-by-step as you heal from sexualization and the impact it has had on your life. Start living a life free of sexualization and objectification today!

Intrigue Addiction

$29.95

The intrigue addict is constantly searching for a look or gesture from another person that insinuates they are attracted to or interested in them. Dr. Weiss explains the depths of intrigue addiction and gives practical steps to take ownership of these behaviors and rid yourself of them.

SERIES FOR MEN

Clean: A Proven Plan For Men Committed to Sexual Integrity

BOOK: $16.99/DVD: $29.95/JOURNAL: $14.99

Clean is a priceless, no-nonsense resource for every husband, father, brother, son, friend, pastor, and Christian leader on the front lines of this war. It is a soldier's handbook for those ready to reclaim their homes, churches, and nations for the God who has built them to succeed.

Lust Free Living

BOOK: $13.95/DVD: $23.95

Every man can fight for and obtain a lust-free lifestyle. Once you know how to stop lust, you will realize how weak lust really can be. God gave you the power to protect those you love from the ravages of lust for the rest of your life! It's time to take it back!

Men Make Men

DVD: $29.95/GUIDEBOOK: $11.95

Dr. Weiss takes the listeners by the hand and step-by-step walks through the creative process God used to make every man into a man of God. This practical teaching on DVD combined with the *Men Make Guidebook* can revitalize the men in any home or local church.

Sex, Men, and God Book

$14.99

This book sends an encouraging message to men who want to be sexually successful. God is not against sexual pleasure in your marriage. In fact, He created it. So, what is keeping you from experiencing the best of His creation? This book has clearly and creatively outlined practical, doable suggestions and principles that will help you enjoy your sexuality as God intended.

Sex, Men, and God CD

$23.95

This CD shows you that God is not against sexual pleasure in your marriage! In fact, He created it! So, what is keeping you from experiencing the best of His creation? These downloads have clearly and creatively outlined practical, doable suggestions and principles that will help you enjoy your sexuality as God intended.

PRODIGAL PARENT PROCESS RESOURCES

Prodigal Parent Process Full Set

BOOK: $94.85

The Parent Prodigal Process DVD, book, and workbook together unveil several causes for a child being a prodigal and helps you therapeutically work through deep-rooted struggles related to being a parent of a prodigal. Working through this series will prompt serious internal dialogue with yourself as it relates to your prodigal child.

Prodigal Parent Process Book

BOOK: $19.95

Dr. Weiss, drawing upon his thirty-plus years of experience working with prodigals and parents of prodigals, delivers biblical and practical tools to aid you in your journey to hope and healing. You can't change the fact that you have a prodigal, but you can set your mind on how you will go through this journey with your prodigal.

Prodigal Parent Process Workbook

WORKBOOK: $16.95

In conjunction with the *Parent Prodigal Process* videos, this workbook helps you therapeutically work through deep-rooted struggles related to being a parent of a prodigal. Working through this series and workbook will prompt serious internal dialogue with yourself as it relates to your prodigal child.

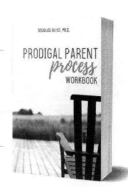

Prodigal Parent Process DVD

DVD: $59.95

Dr. Weiss, drawing upon his thirty-plus years of experience working with prodigals and parents of prodigals, delivers biblical and practical tools to aid you in your journey to hope and healing. You can't change the fact that you have a prodigal, but you can set your mind on how you will go through this journey with your prodigal.

MARRIAGE RESOURCES

Upgrade Your Sex Life

BOOK: $16.95/DVD: $29.95

Upgrade Your Sex Life actually teaches your own unique sexual expression that you and your partner are pre-wired to enjoy. Once you learn what your type is, you can communicate and have sex on a more satisfying level.

Servant Marriage

$16.95

The *Servant Marriage* book is a revelation on God's masterpiece of marriage. In these pages, you will walk with God as He creates the man, the woman, and His masterpiece called marriage.

Marriage Mondays

$59.95

This is an eight week marriage training that actually gives you the skills to have a healthy, more vibrant marriage. Each week Dr. Weiss tackles major aspects of marriage from a biblical perspective. Apply these techniques and it will transform your marriage. This course provides couples to grow their marriages either in a small group setting or as their very own private marriage retreat.

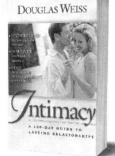

Intimacy: 100 Day Guide to Lasting Relationships

$22.95

The *Intimacy: A 100 Day Guide to Lasting Relationships* book gives you a game plan to improve your relationships. Intimacy doesn't need to be illusive! It's time to recognize intimacy for what it is – a loving and lifelong process that you can learn and develop.

10 Minute Marriage

$14.99

The Ten Minute Marriage Principle refreshes your marriage with quick, daily steps that take 10 minutes daily. Dr. Weiss offers simple exercises in this book that will deepen your marriage and relationship. These exercises include completing statements like: "If I were writing a love letter to you today, it would say..." Dr. Weiss presents a solid insight into fundamental personality differences, sexual likes and dislikes, and establishing an intelligent way to make decisions together.

COUNSELING SERVICES

"Without the intensive, my marriage would have ended, and I would not have known why. Now I am happier than ever, and my marriage is bonded permanently."

Counseling Sessions

Many of our clients start seeing us because they are at a crossroads, struggling with feelings of hopelessness, battling addiction, intimacy anorexia, trauma, or relationship issues. We recognize the courage it takes for you to seek help, and because of this, we have a distinct approach to therapy. We don't just address symptoms; we dive deep to uncover and process the root causes of your unique situation, offering you actionable tools, exercises, and solutions tailored to your needs. Our team understands your challenges, and we are here to provide practical strategies to process and understand the root of your struggles and help you move forward.

Couples Therapy

Couples therapy sessions provide a safe and collaborative environment for you and your partner to openly address challenges, reestablish trust, and navigate the path toward healing and reconnection with professional guidance.

Individual Therapy

Individual therapy sessions offer a private and focused space where you can explore your unique challenges, receive tailored guidance, and work toward healing and growth with a professional who can help you move forward.

Support Groups

A support group allows you to work through healing resources together and be accountable to others as you are on your recovery journey. We have free local support groups in the Colorado Springs area and host virtual support groups for those not local.

Individual, couples, and Intensive sessions are available virtually or in person at our office in Colorado Springs.

An Intensive Success Story

After their marriage was devastated by affairs, sexual addiction, and intimacy anorexia, Nathaniel and Heather didn't know where to turn. Nathaniel's hopelessness of overcoming these addictions and Heather's trauma from the disclosure seemed like too big of an obstacle to overcome. That's when they contacted Heart to Heart Counseling Center for help. Five years post-intensive, they open up about their transformative experience.

For more information visit www.drdougweiss.com or call 719.278.3708

ACCELERATE YOUR HEALING WITH COUNSELING INTENSIVES

"The 5-day intensive exceeded all of my expectations. It was tailored to our particular needs. I truly believe I'm in the midst of a miracle and credit God and this program, Dr. Weiss, and Heart to Heart counseling center (the entire staff), from what I heard, are phenomenal."

We offer customized intensives to cater to your specific needs. Through our deep-dive approach, we aim to identify the root cause of your problems and provide you with the necessary tools to accelerate your healing and recovery in a three or five-day intensive program. Our therapeutic intensive experience is in-person at our office in Colorado Springs, Colorado.

Starting your personal journey toward healing can be as easy as scheduling a counseling session with us today.

3 and 5 Day Intensives

in Colorado Springs, Colorado are available for the following issues:

- Past Trauma
- Parents of Prodigals
- Marital Issues
- Partner Betrayal Trauma
- Affair Recovery
- Intimacy issues

Our Trauma Intensives can be a lifeline for individuals grappling with a range of traumas, such as:

- **Childhood Abuse/Neglect:** Addressing the emotional wounds caused by abuse and a lack of proper care and attention during formative years.
- **Sexual Trauma:** Providing a safe space to heal from the devastating effects of sexual abuse or assault.
- **Family of Origin Issues:** Exploring and healing from dysfunctional family dynamics that continue to affect your present life.
- **Loss and Grief:** Guiding you through the process of coping with loss, whether it's a loved one, a relationship, or a life transition.
- **Emotional Abuse:** Helping you recognize and heal from the scars left by psychological manipulation and control.
- **Abandonment and Rejection:** Supporting you in overcoming the pain and insecurities of feeling abandoned or rejected by loved ones.

For more information visit www.drdougweiss.com or call 719.278.3708

A·A·S·A·T

American Association for Sex Addiction Therapy

Over the course of this training, you will learn how to knowledgeably and effectively help sex addicts, intimacy anorexics, and those married to sex addicts or intimacy anorexics. This program has helped many professionals change thousands of lives and will help to certify you as a pastor, coach, or therapist.

Supervision is a distinguishing part of our program. Supervision is performed weekly via teleconference with Dr. Doug Weiss, one of the leading experts in the field of sex addiction, intimacy anorexia, and partner betrayal trauma. This part of our program allows you to utilize your training and skills together. You will be able to connect and network with other professionals and have your questions answered through this supervision process.

Sex Addiction Training Set

$1,195

Now more than ever, both men and women are seeking counsel for sexually addictive behaviors. You can be prepared! Forty-seven hours of topics related to sexual addiction treatment are covered in this training including:

- The Six Types of Sex Addicts
- Sex and Recovery
- Neurological Understanding
- Relapse Prevention Strategies

Partner's Recovery Training Set

$995

With this AASAT training, you will gain proven clinical insight into treating the issues facing partners. You can be prepared! Thirty-nine hours of topics related to partners treatment are covered in this training, including:

- Partner Model
- Anger
- Partner Grief
- Boundaries

Intimacy Anorexia Training Set

$995

Intimacy Anorexia mental health professionals are needed in your community. Now, you can be prepared to identify it and treat it. In this training you'll cover topics like:

- Identifying Intimacy Anorexia
- Treatment Plan
- Causes of Intimacy Anorexia
- Relapse Strategies

For more information, visit aasat.org or call 719.330.2425

Struggling with Trauma, Anxiety, and PTSD?

Trauma, anxiety, and PTSD can imbalance your brain. When your brain is out of balance or stuck, you don't feel right, and it's impossible to function at your highest level. Cereset is a proven technology that's non-invasive and highly effective. Cereset can help your brain free itself, enabling you to achieve higher levels of well-being and balance throughout your life.

Cereset – Garden of the Gods is located at Heart to Heart Counseling Center in Colorado Springs, Colorado, and specializes in working with sexual addiction, intimacy anorexia, betrayal trauma, PTSD, anxiety, and more.

Here's what clients had to say about Cereset Garden of the Gods after their sessions:

"Cereset helped save our marriage. My husband and I both did Cereset, and it helped both of us be calmer and sleep better; we responded to each other in a more loving and respectful way. I notice a big change in him, and he says the same about me. After the sessions, I noticed a marked improvement in my sleep and my ability to stay calm during moments that would trigger an argument with my spouse prior to Cereset. Before Cereset, we felt chaotic, and now, afterward, we both feel more at peace. Our household is a calm place to be now, and we are so grateful!"

"I've noticed a significant improvement in my ability to control and correct my patterns of thought – specifically negative thoughts. I also noticed my reaction to negative events was calmer and more controlled instead of being thrown in a downward spiral. I'm more able to recognize and deal with stress."

"As a health care provider, I would refer patients for Cereset. I suffered from extreme sleeplessness and difficulty falling asleep and staying asleep. I did not sleep more than 2-3 hours a night for years. By the week's end, I slept 7 hours a night! I also suffered from extreme anxiety and PTSD, which, after years, led to depression and feelings of hopelessness/helplessness. My anxiety has significantly improved. You were amazing, professional, knowledgeable, and tailored to my needs very well. Cereset produces results. If you are on the fence about this, trust the evidence-based studies and the thousands of positive testimonials. You will NOT regret it."

View a client testimonial here

Schedule Your Cereset Intensive Today!

The cost for five sessions (one per day) is $1,500.

For more information call us at 719-644-5778

Made in the USA
Columbia, SC
14 June 2024

36629628R00065